A Note from the Author

We all know that good feeling we get when someone is kind to us.
And we also know that good feeling we get when we are kind to others.
Sharing, caring, and giving are acts of kindness that bless both the giver
and the receiver.

Many young children have tender, sensitive spirits and a desire to
help others, but they often think they are too young to make a difference,
or they are too shy to reach out to others. Parents and teachers can teach
their children that they can help others by simply being kind, thoughtful,
and caring, and that God can use their acts of kindness to make a difference
in someone's life.

> *And that's how kindness starts!*
> *When someone cares and someone gives*
> *it blesses people's hearts.*

Encourage young children to respond to someone
who has a need. Remind them that even though
others may not notice the kind things that they do,

> *God sees every single time*
> *and He is pleased with you.*

Showing kindness to our friends,
family members, or people we happen
to meet, is a way to honor our
heavenly Father who tells us to set
an example for others even
when we're young.
(1 Timothy 4:12).

Crystal Bowman

To my dear mother, Gerene Langejans—
you have touched many lives with your kindness, thoughtfulness, and caring.
You set an example for others.
—C.B.

Published by Standard Publishing, Cincinnati, Ohio
www.standardpub.com

Text Copyright © 2010 by Crystal Bowman
Illustrations Copyright © 2010 by Standard Publishing

Printed November 2009 in Shenzhen, Guangdong, China.
Project editor: Ruth Frederick
Illustrator: Karen Lee
Cover & interior design: Suzanne Jacobson

ISBN 978-0-7847-2397-5

Library of Congress Cataloging-in-Publication Data

Bowman, Crystal.
  The boy on the yellow bus / written by Crystal Bowman ; illustrated by Karen Lee.
     p. cm.
  Summary: When a young boy invites a new student to share his seat on the bus, he triggers a chain reaction of kind acts that reach throughout their school and beyond.
  ISBN 978-0-7847-2397-5
  [1. Kindness--Fiction. 2. Schools--Fiction. 3. Christian life--Fiction.] I. Lee, Karen (Karen Jones), 1961- ill. II. Title.
  PZ8.3.B6773Bpe 2010
  [E]--dc22
                            2009031961

15 14 13 12 11 10   1 2 3 4 5 6 7 8 9

The Boy on the Yellow Bus

Written by
Crystal Bowman

Illustrated by
Karen Lee

Standard
PUBLISHING

Cincinnati, Ohio

Sam got on the yellow bus.
Sam was new in town.
He didn't know where he should go,
or where he should sit down.

His hands were getting sweaty.
His face was turning red.
"You can sit here next to me,"
a young boy kindly said.

Sam was very happy
to share the young boy's seat.
"Thanks!" he said. "It's hard to be
the new kid on the street."

When Sam got off the yellow bus,
he met a girl named Sue.
She dropped her lunch box in the mud.
Sam knew what he could do.

He picked it up and wiped it off.
    "Hey, thanks a lot!" she said.
Sue was very happy that
    she didn't have soggy bread!

At noon Sue opened up her lunch.
She had good things to eat—
    a sandwich and an apple,
    and some cookies for a treat.

But Brian only had some bread.
    Sue knew what she could do.
She said, "I've got a cookie
    that I'd like to share with you."

"I like cookies!" Brian said.
Then he went out to play.
The kids were playing soccer
on the soccer field that day.

But Brian saw that Kim was sad
and sitting on the side.
"What's the matter?" Brian asked.
Then Kim looked down and cried.

"The kids won't let me play with them,
and some are being mean."
So Brian hollered to his friends,
"Hey! Kim is on my team!"

Kim jumped up and joined the team,
then she began to run.
She helped to score the winning goal
before the game was done!

Kim was busy after school.
She had a lot to do—
   like ride her bike and play with friends
   and feed her goldfish too.

But Kim saw that her mother
   was working very hard,
and so Kim helped to pull the weeds
   and tidy up the yard.

And that's the way the whole day went—
and that's how kindness starts.
When someone cares and someone gives
it blesses people's hearts.

God tells us in the Bible
    that we should help and share.
It only takes a little time
    to show someone we care.

So share your seat or share your lunch,
and help somebody out.

That's what love and kindness
are really all about.

Sometimes people never see
the good things that you do.
But God sees every single time,
and He is pleased with you.

You can do important things,
no matter what your size.
And when you're kind to others,
you're a hero in God's eyes.

Crystal Bowman has written over 60 books for kids. Her books come in all shapes and sizes and many of them have become best sellers. Whether her stories are written in playful rhythm and rhyme, or short sentences for beginning readers, she tries to make them so enjoyable that kids will want to read them over and over again. She also writes lyrics for children's piano music, magazine articles, teacher resource materials, and devotional books. She is a national speaker and has been a guest on numerous Christian radio programs as well as local television programs. She lives in Palm Beach Gardens, Florida where she loves to go for walks on the beach.

Karen Lee has illustrated several books for children, is a frequent art contributor to *Highlights* magazine, and is the author and illustrator of *ABC Safari*. She lives with her family in Cary, North Carolina.